HORSEMEN
OF THE WESTERN PLATEAUS

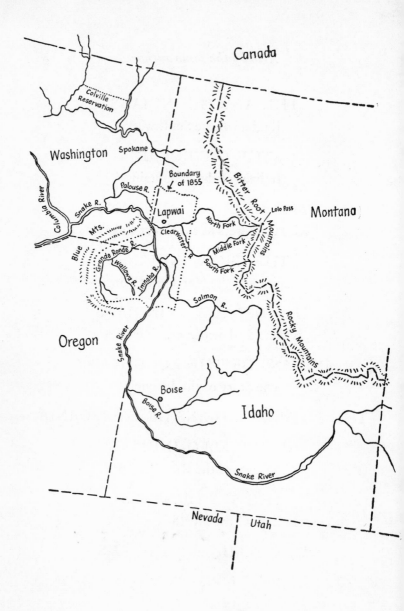

HORSEMEN
OF THE
WESTERN PLATEAUS
·
THE NEZ PERCE INDIANS

By Sonia Bleeker

Illustrated by Patricia Boodell

WILLIAM MORROW AND COMPANY
New York · 1957

Second Printing, May 1960

Library of Congress Catalog Card Number: 57-5111

CONTENTS

Grateful recognition is given to Dr. Verne F. Ray, Department of Anthropology, University of Washington, Seattle, Washington, for reading and criticizing the manuscript.

I

CHANGING TIMES

Spotted Salmon lay on his bunk, wriggling his toes toward the warmth of the fire. His slender brown body was only a shade lighter than the buffalo robe under him. He liked to rest this way and watch Mother prepare the evening meal. His own share of the daily chores was done. He had caught the salmon for tonight's meal and had

11

helped Mother gather firewood. Now, like the men in their large house, he wanted to rest before the evening meal.

The warmth of the fire enveloped his body. Spotted Salmon smoothed the dry, woolly buffalo hair of the robe with his fingers and looked up into the blue sky above the smoke holes in the roof. It was still light outside. Inside, the corners of the large house were already shadowed with darkness. The sun was ending another day's journey, sinking to rest behind the mountains. Like me, Spotted Salmon thought, Sun, too, is tired.

Stretched to his full height, Spotted Salmon was already as tall as some of the men in the long-house, although he was only fifteen. His people were the Nez Perce (nez-purse) Indians, who lived on the plateaus in what is now western Idaho and eastern Oregon and Washington. *Nez Perce* means *pierced noses* in French. The name was given to these Indians by French fur traders early in the seventeenth century. It may be that in those days, when the French traders first came to the American Northwest, some of these Indians had their noses pierced by a long piece of bone or shell drilled through a hole in the cartilage between the nostrils. They believed this made a person look handsome and different. However, in Spotted Salmon's day, the beginning of the nineteenth century, pierced noses were almost unknown among these people. Yet the name, Nez Perce, still stuck to them.

Spotted Salmon raised himself slightly and pulled a roll of beaver pelts under his head for a pillow. Thus propped up, he had a better view of the whole house, which his family shared with four other families. All the people in this large house were Spotted Salmon's relatives: his grandmother and grandfather; grandfather's brother and his wife, whom Spotted Salmon called grandfather and grandmother, too; and Father's brothers' families. In some of the other longhouses in the small village, ten and twelve families lived together. Usually two families shared one of the fires that were aligned in the center of the house.

Everywhere in our village, Spotted Salmon thought, men are resting now, while mothers are preparing the evening meals, with their daughters helping them.

Right now, in the large house at the edge of the village, Sunflower Girl was helping her mother, too. Spotted Salmon had given her the second fish he had caught that day. In his thoughts Spotted Salmon always saw Sunflower Girl on horseback. She was the best rider among all the girls in the village. Spotted Salmon often raced with her while she was tending her father's horses in the meadows outside their village.

Spotted Salmon's own mother was unhurried and quiet, just like Sunflower Girl. In her long buckskin dress, fringed at the sleeves and hem, and her soft moccasins, Mother glided softly across the mats that covered the floor. She usually wore a little rounded cap with a tassel, that looked like an upside-down basket. She removed it when she worked indoors, and her hair, parted in the middle and flattened by the cap, was smooth and glossy. She had all her cooking utensils near her at the firepit: her large, tightly woven cooking baskets, the wooden serving bowls and ladles, the spoons made of horn, and the large woven water basket. Her little pile of smooth stones to be used in boiling food were being heated in the ashes. The large, flat stones for broiling and baking were stacked close to the firepit.

Everything was now ready. The fish was cleaned and cut into two strips. Mother impaled them on two sticks and put them to broil over the hot ashes. The dried brown camas (kah'-mahs) that looked like bits of brown bark but tasted sweet, had been soaking in a wooden bowl filled with water. The women dug up the camas bulbs in the meadows in early spring and fall.

Now Mother raked several heated stones from the ashes. She poured water into one of her cooking baskets. Then, after dipping the hot stones into the wooden bowl to clean them, she threw them into the cooking basket. The water began to bubble.

The woman who shared the firepit with Mother sat down opposite her and raked several hot stones out of her side of the pit. The women spoke to each other in their soft Shahaptian speech—the language of the Nez Perce. The women's long braids kept slipping across their shoulders as they bent over their cooking. With quick movements of their heads and shoulders, they tossed the braids back into place and busily stirred the food with long-handled ladles.

Spotted Salmon wondered whether Mother would eat tonight. Now that spring had come and the Month of Flowers (March) was half over, she ate more sparingly than usual. On some days, Spotted Salmon suspected, she fasted all day long, so the spirits would pity her and listen to her prayers for Father's safety.

Mother and her two sisters-in-law were expecting the men back from a trading trip. Several moons ago, Father had gone over the mountains in the direction of the rising sun, to trade horses for buffalo skins and meat. There, in the east, lay a flat land with herds of buffalo. The buffalo hunters, the Indians of the plains, always needed horses. Twice each year Nez Perce Indians set out for the buffalo country to trade their horses. Father and his two brothers were due back now.

Mother, like all the Nez Perce, believed that if she followed certain rules set up by her guardian spirit this spirit would help her husband. It did not matter how far away Father was or what he was doing, her spirit helper would reach him. When she was a young girl, Mother, like other Nez Perce children, had gone up alone on a mountainside to pray there for a dream or a vision. Her vision turned out to be a blackbird, one of the birds that follow the buffalo and feed on the flies and insects infesting them. The buffalo welcome these blackbirds, and the birds are not afraid of the enormous beasts. Wherever buffalo feed, they are usually accompanied by a swarm of these small, cheerful birds perching on the buffalos' backs and hopping in front of them, looking for insects and seeds.

Mother had seen these birds when first she went to the plains with her father to trade. She

could not forget them. When a blackbird came to her in her vision, she thought of it as her guardian spirit. And Mother's parents had named her Blackbird. Mother was sure that her guardian spirit in the land of the buffalo would help Father. So she prayed to it.

The two other women, who did not own good medicine, could be of very little help to their husbands. But Mother had powerful medicine. She was expected to help her husband by using this medicine in many ways.

Watching Mother, Spotted Salmon knew she was keeping her thoughts on her guardian spirit. This was the same as praying and asking for help. Mother had hesitated to go with Father on this trip, because his parents were too old for the long journey. Grandfather did not want to die in a strange country. He wanted his spirit to leave him in the Nez Perce lands, on the banks of the Wallowa River, where he was born. Besides, the Nez Perce were not buffalo hunters. They were mainly fishermen, and hunters of elk and deer. Grandfather did not want to change his ways so late in life and become a wanderer, a follower of the buffalo trails. Yet the people needed the skins and robes the men brought back from the plains.

They were also hungry for meat, especially after the long winter. So Father and his two brothers had left without their families. Spotted Salmon was old enough to go, but Father had wanted him to stay at home to take care of the horses.

The boy looked at his father's empty bunk, stripped of its buffalo robe and beaver skins. During the past cold months, Grandfather had used Father's robe. With a pang, Spotted Salmon realized how much he wanted Father home.

As yet Spotted Salmon had said nothing to Sunflower Girl about his feelings for her. He felt she liked him. But he would have to speak to her father first and give him a few horses, so she would know that he wanted her for his wife. It was customary among the Nez Perce to give the father of a girl a gift before a young man could ask to marry his daughter. However, all horses belonged to Father, and Spotted Salmon could not give any away without his consent. He was afraid some other young man might speak to Sunflower Girl's father in the meantime.

Being a Nez Perce, the son of a hunter, Spotted Salmon did not waste too much time in daydreams. Instead, he firmly reached overhead into a large storage basket where he kept his work. He pulled out an unfinished length of horsehair rope and began to braid it, tying one end to the pole near his bunk and pulling the rope taut as he worked. Father needed horsehair ropes for the horses. Spotted Salmon had already made many fine ones which Father took with him to trade. The boy collected the horsehair himself. The Nez Perce let their horses' manes and tails grow very long. He combined the gray and the black hair into pleasing stripes and attractive zigzag lines.

Grandfather always said that work made the day seem short. Spotted Salmon had barely finished a finger's length of rope when Mother called, "Food is ready." Quickly he got up, squatted on a mat by Mother's side, and picked up his spoon, made from the horn of a bighorn sheep. He waited politely till his mother took a

few mouthfuls of the camas before dipping his spoon into the serving bowl. The broiled fish was now cool enough to eat, and Spotted Salmon bit into his slice.

The meal was not enough to fill a hungry boy. Spotted Salmon could have eaten twice as much. He had had only a few mouthfuls of hot camas cakes that Mother had boiled for his morning meal, and nothing since. But the fish he had brought home was a small one.

The salmon will come up the Wallowa River a few moons from now, he thought, as he ate. There will be enough food for everyone then. Right now fishing is poor; the fish are small.

The other families in the longhouse also ate sparingly, since they were getting low on stored food—the plants and berries they had dried and stored last fall. But winter was over and soon there would be good, tasty camas and kouse (kah'-oos) bulbs for everyone.

The boy got up and went to his bunk again. Mother wiped the horn spoons and wooden serv-

ing bowl clean with dried sage, and covered the
fire with ashes. There was still light coming in
through the smoke holes, and Spotted Salmon
continued braiding the horsehair rope. Mother
sat down on her bunk and took out her work. She
was making a bag of Indian hemp.

Indian hemp grew wild everywhere in the
river valleys. The women gathered it and
pounded the stalks to separate the fibers. Then
they spun the fibers into thread and the thread
into cord. The bags were twined, as one twines
a basket, and were covered with designs of color-
ful embroidery. These woven bags were very
handsome. They lasted a long time and were in
great demand in trading.

After putting her children to bed, Spotted
Salmon's aunt came over and sat down near
Mother on the bed. She brought her work with
her. Aunt was also making a bag, but it was very
small. "It's for my daughter," Aunt said. "She
wants to carry a bag just like mine when we leave
for the camas meadows."

Like Mother, Aunt was anxious about her husband's return, but neither spoke about her man. It was not a good thing to speak of the men at this time of the evening. Thinking of the men might disturb them, wherever they were, and make them lose sleep. Men on the trail needed their sleep. So the women talked about the weather, about spring, and the coming trip to the meadows to gather camas. Mother pointed to the storage baskets she had prepared for the trip and the bags she had made. "We shall need much food soon," she said. Under other circumstances, she would have said, "When the men come." But the return of the men remained unmentioned.

"My children can't wait to go," Aunt said. "I'll have to keep them from eating too much raw camas. Something evil entered their bodies last fall when they ate so much raw camas. Both were ill. I had to wake their grandmother late in the night and start the fire going so she could brew a drink for them. It was fortunate she had brought those good herbs that cure stomach-aches."

"Grandmother cured Spotted Salmon, too, when he was little and had eaten too much raw camas. I always carry some of the herbs Grandmother gathers and dries," Mother said.

"When I finish with this bag," Aunt continued, "I am going to make two good digging sticks."

Men were gathering in the far end of the house. Spotted Salmon picked up his buckskin pillow. He heard Mother say, as he was leaving, "Last spring Son helped me with the digging. Now that he is so big, he will not help. He will say it is women's work."

"My oldest might be a help with the camas this time," Aunt said. "He was too little last fall, but he is willing."

"With Spotted Salmon it is always horses, horses, and horses. He doesn't even want to go fishing any more," Mother complained.

"It is so with all the boys," Aunt agreed, as she wound more hemp. "Nobody wants to go fishing any more. All the boys want is to race around on horseback, to go to the plains, and to go to war. Times are changing."

Spotted Salmon sat down beside two other boys and prepared to listen. None of the men remained idle. The two old men in the gathering, Grandfather and Grandfather's brother, lighted their pipes and took a few puffs. The three young men who made up the rest of the gathering had just returned from the south. Each had in his hands some tool, made either of bone or stone, and each was chipping, scraping, or notching something. They were working on arrowheads, fishhooks, stone hammers, wedges, and clubs.

Grandfather had finished making a war club and was now carving a design on it, to which he would later add color prepared with various earth dyes. Spotted Salmon knew the club was for Father, even though Grandfather did not say so. But he had been working on it with great care and patience for many days.

It will be worth a buffalo robe, Spotted Salmon thought, as he started braiding another rope.

Grandfather's brother, who was a shaman (shah'man)—that is, a medicine man—was busy smoothing and shaping feathers for his prayer sticks. The men began to talk about horses, and the boys listened attentively.

At this time, the beginning of the nineteenth century, just before the Lewis and Clark Expedition visited them, the Nez Perce owned large herds of horses. They were very proud of these herds, which were famous among the Indian tribes, especially among the plains tribes. The Nez Perce had traded and raided horses from the south for almost a century. The Spaniards, of course, had brought horses to this continent. There were no horses in the Americas before the Spaniards came.

The plateau lands of the Nez Perce, part forest and part prairie, with many mountain streams and rivers, proved excellent for horse breeding. Although the summers were hot and dry, the winters in the river valleys were mild and almost free of snow. Horses remained on the open range the year round. There was always enough food for them. Wolves, the enemies of horses, were rare in the Nez Perce lands. A horse can fight off a wolf or a wild dog, but a colt cannot. On the plains, where both wolves and wild dogs abounded, they killed many colts. But in the shelter of the Bitterroot Mountains, where the Nez Perce lived, the colts were safe, so the herds of horses grew rapidly. From their neighbors to the south and east, the Nez Perce first learned to care for horses and to ride them. Within a dozen years after horses first came to their lands, the Nez Perce young men became excellent horsemen and riders.

White horses and particularly those that had spots on their rumps were especially liked. War chiefs felt more important when they rode white horses, and horses with spots on their rumps were also preferred in trading. The Nez Perce kept these spotted horses apart and interbred them. These began to be called Appaloosa horses, after the Palouse River. The Appaloosas were known for their hardiness, speed, and gentleness. In the fall Spotted Salmon's father had taken several Appaloosas with him to the plains.

While Father was away trading, Spotted Salmon's job was to ride out daily to check on the herd. The Nez Perce had not yet begun to brand their horses. However, Spotted Salmon knew each horse in Father's herd and could single it out from among Father's brothers' horses. The herd grazed together. Already several mares had foaled and their colts were prancing about, feeding and playing. Spotted Salmon's favorite, a white Appaloosa mare, swift and gentle, had foaled a beautiful spotted colt. The boy could not wait to show it off to Father.

Eagle Claw was talking now. He was a young man, only two or three winters older than Spotted Salmon. However, he had just returned from a raid for horses and so had the right to speak; and the older men listened. Eagle Claw and another young man from the village had joined several men from the Nez Perce villages along the

Wallowa River and formed a raiding party with their friends, the Flatheads, who lived to the north. They had gone south to Shoshoni country.

Eagle Claw had told his story before, but it was customary for a man to repeat a story over and over before a circle of men. No one tired of this repetition, since it helped them memorize the details. In this way, listening to the experi-

ence of others, men learned and gained in wisdom.
Men and boys wanted to know about the country
through which they might some day travel, about
the villages that dotted the valleys. They wanted
to know who was friendly to the Nez Perce and
who was not.

Among many Indian groups strangers were
regarded with suspicion. To raid a stranger's
camp was as good as a victory on the warpath.
However, after they had met a stranger and
particularly after he had smoked the pipe with
the men of a village, he became a friend. Often
the horses raided from a stranger were returned
on the morning after such a meeting. As a friend,
the newcomer was given the best protection and
advice.

It often happened that newcomers passing
through Nez Perce lands were raided by other
travelers. When the Nez Perce heard of this, they
often went on the warpath to protect their new
friends. The Nez Perce were known as fighters.
People passing through their lands were anxious

to make friends with each village and equally anxious to treat others in these lands with consideration. No one wanted to provoke a fight with the Nez Perce men.

Eagle Claw was telling his story once again. The Nez Perce and Flathead raiders had been in strange country. Things began to look suspicious, so they dismounted and hid in a clump of trees. They heard several coyote calls, then several bird calls. These calls came so regularly that the raiders began to suspect they were enemy signals and meant that they had been sighted. In the morning, when Eagle Claw was getting his horse ready, a scout had shouted something. Eagle Claw was not sure just what the scout shouted, because he had not learned to understand everything in the Flatheads' language. Anyway, the yell was an alarm, so he and his companion quickly got their things together, threw the packs on their horses, and cautiously walked them out of the woods.

Soon they saw a large herd of horses. There

were enough for the chief of the party and several
for each of the raiders. In the distance they could
see only a few riders. These were definitely
Shoshoni. The raiders could tell this by the way
they carried their bows and arrows and their
shields. The Flathead chief said they should
make a dash after the Shoshoni. He began to
strip himself of his buckskin shirt and feathers.

"Why are you taking those off?" Eagle Claw
asked him. "What are you doing?" The chief
explained that if the Shoshoni saw his feathers

and dress they would know that he was the chief and would go for him first. In a raiding party the men took their orders from the chief. He planned the raid and everyone had to obey him. When a chief was killed, his men often turned back. Hence, in any meeting of raiding parties, men tried to kill or capture the chief first.

"Let me wear them," Eagle Claw begged. "I am not afraid."

Wearing the chief's feathers and shirt, Eagle Claw rushed ahead of the others and raced through the lines of the Shoshoni riders. "They shot at me," he cried, his chest swelling with pride in his own daring. "I did it five times!"

The Nez Perce liked doing things in fives, because they thought five a lucky number. Other Indian groups liked to do things in fours, because to them four was lucky—just as we like to do things in threes because we think three is lucky.

"I faced the enemy and let my arrows fly," Eagle Claw went on. "My friend, who is no longer with us, followed me. He received the Shoshoni arrows, which killed him."

Having killed a man, the Shoshoni scattered fast and disappeared into a canyon. They left a number of horses behind, which Eagle Claw's party caught. The men roamed about till dark, searching for the enemy, then they turned homeward with the horses they had captured. Now Eagle Claw was waiting for warm weather, and the men's return from the plains, to get a raiding party together and go after the Shoshoni to avenge his companion's death.

"I am not afraid of being killed," he repeated. "My friend's spirit will wander until it has been avenged. We must avenge him, so his spirit may find rest."

It was getting late. The fires in the firepits were all covered for the night. The old men got up and went to their bunks to sleep. Spotted Salmon walked back in the dark toward his bed. Mother was already asleep under her buckskin blanket.

Father's bed no longer looked empty. It was covered with his buffalo robe, and at its head lay the buckskin stuffed with hair that he liked to use for a pillow.

Father will be home soon, Spotted Salmon thought. We will go hunting together. We will ask Eagle Claw to take me with him into Shoshoni country. Spotted Salmon's last thought before he fell asleep was, as always, of Sunflower Girl. That white mare and the new colt would be a fine gift for her father. . . . Sunflower Girl loved the mare and her colt as much as he did.

2

THE NEZ PERCE WORLD

The Nez Perce were fishermen and hunters, not farmers. Yet about half their food was plant food. The women and girls gathered it and prepared this vegetable food for eating—either fresh or dried.

Through centuries of watching trees and shrubs, grasses and flowers, unfold with the seasons, mature, and die, the people learned a great deal about plant life. This knowledge they passed on from mother to daughter, from grandmother to granddaughter. By now they were familiar with every plant and shrub that grew in their lands. Many of these they used for curing the sick.

The Nez Perce calendar, as Spotted Salmon heard it and learned it from the people about him

—just as he learned everything else—was made up from the life story of plants. The calendar names show the importance of each season in the daily life of the Nez Perce people.

Like ourselves, the Nez Perce divided the year into four seasons:

Spring	*Etaiyam*
Summer	*Taiyam*
Fall	*Sahnim*
Winter	*Enim*

The months were named as follows:

January	The mid-time of cold weather in Shahaptian—*Wilupup*
February	The month of swelling buds—*Alatamal*
March	The month of flowers—*Latital*
April	The month of kakit. Kakit was a favorite root used as food, which the women dug in April—*Kakital*
May	The month of kouse bread—*Apaal*
June	The month of the first salmon run—*Hillal*
July	The month of eels. At this time the eels followed the salmon up the rivers—*Hazoal*
August	The month of hot weather—*Taiyaal*

September — The month of spawning salmon at the heads of creeks—*Wauwama aiakal*

October — The month of the spawning salmon on Snake River—*Aiakal pikunme*

November — The month when the tamarack trees lose their needles—*Hoplal*

December — The beginning of cold weather or the time of the deer hunts—*Sahliwali*

It was early *Latital* now (March). It was still cold, but the sun carried the promise of spring in its warmth. The old people, wrapped in their buffalo robes and buckskins, liked to sit in the afternoon outside the longhouses, warming themselves in the sun. The dark longhouses let in very little sun and warmth. By now everyone awaited with impatience the home-coming of the men from the buffalo country. Yet the camas bulbs were ready. The Peacetime Chief of the village talked it over with the people. They decided to leave for the meadows. The men would know where to find them, since they always dug for camas in the same places.

Formerly the women and girls, laden with

mats and burden baskets, trudged on foot to the meadows twice a year. The return trips were even harder, because then the burden baskets were full. Now that the Nez Perce had horses, these trips were pleasanter for everyone, especially for the women. They loaded their mats, sleeping robes, and burden baskets, their children and cradleboards on pack horses. Older children rode with their mothers. Those who did not have enough horses doubled up with relatives.

The hunting, like the fishing, was still poor at this time of the year. Hunters did not like to shoot elk cows and does, since most of them had young. The young would perish without the milk and care of their mothers. Besides, the elk and deer shot at this time were still too lean from the sparse winter grazing. The best hunting was in the fall, after the animals had fattened on spring and summer feeding. However, there were rivers and creeks near the meadows. The men and boys could set out their beaver traps, and they could fish.

Spotted Salmon rounded up three pack horses, and the white mare for Mother. The rest of the herd remained in the valley. Grandfather would watch out for the horses. The boy rode his own Appaloosa and led two of the pack horses, while Mother rode the white mare and led the third pack horse. The little colt followed them. Spotted Salmon was happy to have the white mare and her colt along. He would give them special care while they were away from the herd.

Within a short time after they arrived at the camas meadows, the women had their small tipis all set up. They unrolled the robes and made up the beds over a base of brush and grass, and they dug small firepits inside. Everyone retired early, so as to be up with the sun to start digging the camas. The last act of each woman before retiring was to inspect her digging sticks and place them near her.

Mother looked hers over, too. These digging sticks were about as long as a man's arm—two and and a half feet. Mother had hardened the end of

her stick by putting it into the fire and scraping off the burnt wood, till the stick had the sharp point she liked. The point had a slight outward curve. The handle crossed the top end of the digging stick. Mother's handle was made of horn. Other women made their handles of bone or stone. In digging, Mother grasped both ends of the handle and pressed downward. In spring the ground was still moist and soft from the winter's rains, and the digging was not hard. But each woman wanted many basketfuls of camas. To dig up such a quantity took a long time.

The camas, with their lilylike bulbs, grow close together. When in bloom, blue and white flowers cover the erect stalks that grow to three feet in height. Between ten to forty flowers are on a single stalk, making a very dense growth. In spring the camas meadows look like a blue lake, rimmed by green grassy banks. The Nez Perce always stopped to admire the sight. They were

sorry to have to break up the beauty of Mother Earth. But they needed the camas for food.

With their slender digging sticks, the women and girls worked hour after hour dislodging the bulbs. Camas bulbs are edible when raw. The children removed the brown outer skins and ate the crunchy, sweetish, juicy bulbs. Raw camas tasted to the Nez Perce much as raw turnips taste to us.

As the day wore on, the women tired. The children became bored with picking up the bulbs their mothers had dug. They found excuses to run down to the creek to play. To keep them from being bored and from running away, the women talked to them, teaching them about the plants, pointing out the way they grew, the way the leaves were unfolding. Some of the women told the children stories.

Always the stories began with the doings of Coyote. In the Nez Perce legends, Coyote was the chief of all the animals. It was Coyote who named the people as they came up from underground, where they once lived, and spread over the earth. Having named all the people, Coyote ran out of names. He could think of only one word as a name for himself, Coyote. This was not a good name. In fact, it was disliked, but Coyote could think of nothing else. So he named himself Coyote.

Coyote had powerful medicine and could turn himself into anything else he chose to be. He was, like all of us, a combination of wisdom gained from long experience and silliness due to thoughtlessness or just plain mischief.

A favorite story was about how Coyote lost his eyes. This story had spread among many Indian groups of the Northwest, as well as to the plains. It always made everyone laugh. Mother told it the first afternoon of the camas digging. Her sister-in-law's little girl was getting tired. Spotted Salmon had just carried away two full burden baskets of camas. Another little girl came over and the two children began to throw the bulbs at each other, instead of putting them into the empty basket. As Mother began to talk, the little girls promptly squatted down near her digging stick, their busy fingers scraping the dirt off the bulbs as Mother dislodged them.

Coyote was restless, as usual. He wanted to go and do something, so he set out on a journey. On his way he heard a wildcat singing a song:

> "O my eyes, come back!
> O my eyes, come back!"

Coyote looked up and saw two eyes, like tiny birds, floating in the air. He recognized the bright, tawny eyes of Wildcat. "What a trick!" he exclaimed. "I must try and do the same with my eyes."

It hurt him very much, but finally Coyote pulled one eye out and threw it up in the air. Then he took out his other eye and threw it into the air. Coyote was suddenly in total darkness. He cried out in pain:

"O my eyes, come back!
O my eyes, come back!"

Nothing happened. Coyote remained in total darkness. He did not see Wildcat sneak up, pick up his eyes as they fell to the ground, and run off with them. For a long time Coyote kept calling for his eyes. Then he fell asleep and, after a long while, woke up again. He pricked his elbow and a little boy stepped out. Coyote told the little boy to lead him in search of people.

The first man they met was very big; but with the little boy's help Coyote overcame him, threw him to the ground, took out his eyes, and put them into his own sockets. Now that he could see again, Coyote made the little boy disappear. He promised the man that he would soon return and give him back his eyes. "They will be a little red around the rims," Coyote warned the man, "because you are bleeding, but I'll fix them so you will see at night as well as you do in the daytime." The blinded man smiled with joy. To be able to see at night as well as in the daytime would make him the most powerful hunter and fisherman in the world. He lay back patiently to await Coyote's return.

Coyote wandered all day. He was hungry when he knocked at the first hut in a village. Inside he could hear a woman singing a victory song:

> "Hi ye ye a he!
> Hi ye ye a he!"

Coyote quickly changed himself into an old man and entered the hut. The woman was grinding sunflower seeds into flour as she sang.

"What makes you so happy?" Coyote asked.

"Haven't you heard? Coyote has lost his eyes. Now he won't be able to do any more mischief."

"Why are you grinding all this flour?"

"My five daughters are at a dance, celebrating Coyote's misfortune," the woman said happily. "They will soon be home and they are hungry."

So everyone is happy because I lost my eyes,

Coyote thought. In anger, he turned upon the woman. "How short is your memory!" he said with bitterness. "The reason you and your people are alive today is because in ancient times Coyote killed the monster that was eating all the people. You and your people have forgotten how he risked his life and entered the body of that monster. He might have died. Luckily his powers were strong. He cut out the monster's heart and saved all the people."

The woman looked earnestly at Coyote. "No, Grandfather, we have not forgotten the many good things Coyote did. We remember them and we tell them to our children, so they, too, will be grateful to Coyote for his goodness. Saving all the people from the monster was a good deed. No one forgets that. But since then Coyote has done many silly and mischievous things that hurt the people. Now that he has lost his eyes, maybe he will not do them any more."

This reply only added to Coyote's anger. He pushed the woman aside, grabbed the bowl with the ground sunflower seeds, and ate them. Then he carried the woman to the small hut next to her house and changed himself into the woman herself. Imitating her ways, he sat down by the grindstone and pretended to grind the sunflower seeds.

Soon the five daughters entered the house. They were hungry. "Mother, what have you for us to eat?" they asked.

Coyote, imitating the woman's voice, replied: "Daughters, I am not well and could not grind any sunflower seeds for you. Do it yourselves."

"Mother," the girls said as they set to work, "we will take you with us to the dance tomorrow. The chief said that because you are the oldest you may dance with Coyote's eyes during the ceremony."

Next day the daughters carried Coyote to the ceremony. He said he was still ill and could hardly walk. Everybody was at the dance. Wildcat gave the woman Coyote's eyes to dance with. Coyote took his eyes from Wildcat and began to

dance. He looked for an opening in the crowd, found it, and made a dash for it. As he disappeared into the woods, the people realized that the woman was Coyote in disguise.

Time passed quickly when stories were told. The little girls continued working as they listened. They brushed the earth off the dark camas bulbs, placed them in the baskets, and cupped their hands close to the digging stick for another clump of bulbs.

Women and girls followed the same routine in digging kouse roots. These were gathered during the months of April and May. Kouse grew on dry hillsides. In early spring the fragrant rosette of leaves of the kouse plants, peering from the dead stalks and grass, showed the women just where the plants were. The young bulblike roots tasted like turnips. Later on, as the kouse matured, it tasted like celery. Preparing kouse for eating was different from cooking camas. The fresh roots were pounded into small, thin cakes. These cakes the women laid out on mats to dry in the sun. Well dried kouse cakes kept for a long time.

The preparation of camas was more complicated. First, the women removed the dark outer skin from the bulbs. They put the cleaned bulbs in baskets and carried them to the pit for steaming.

The pit was about six feet across and about three feet deep. The entire group shared the same pit, and they used the same pit season after season. First, the women cleaned it of the accumulated brush and debris that had blown in during the winter. When the pit was clean they piled dry wood into it, about a foot high. On top of the wood they laid stones to be heated and set the wood afire.

As soon as the fire burned down, the women reset the red-hot stones so they were level and covered them with a layer of earth and coarse grass. Now each woman emptied her baskets of camas into the pit. Another layer of grass about three inches thick was laid over the camas. The girls poured water over the grass, which at once began to steam. They covered the grass with a layer of sand and let the camas steam for an entire day.

Toward evening of the day following, the women carefully removed the earth and grass and put the steamed, shrunken, browned bulbs into

wooden serving bowls. This first night there
would be a feast of camas. The men and boys,
who had been fishing and trapping, joined the
women. No one bothered dividing the food
among the families present. Everyone just ate
and ate as much as he or she could hold.

At first everyone was silent, enjoying the sweet,
hot food, which they scooped up out of the bowls
with their spoons. They ate quickly at first, then
more and more slowly. Soon Spotted Salmon and
his friends felt full too. Each held on to a few
lumps of camas and nibbled at them, hating to
give up and admit that their stomachs were full.

"Tomorrow after the camas have been put to
steam, let the boys and girls have a game of ball,"
an older woman suggested. Everyone agreed.

The next day, the women and girls were up
with the dawn, as usual. Each worked hard to
fill at least a few baskets before she hurried home
to clean the camas bulbs and carry them over to
the pit to be steamed. Even the small children
hurried home with the elders. They enjoyed a

ball game as much as everyone else, even though they were not old enough to take part in it.

The pit was quickly made ready. The girls had a fire going in no time. The women arranged the hot stones, and the grass and earth were piled on as they had been the day before. When the layers were arranged and water had been poured over them, a last layer of cooked camas was added. This was a layer of camas cakes rolled in grass. They were the leftovers from yesterday's feast. Earlier the girls had pounded these leftovers into a dough and shaped the dough into small cakes. They rolled the cakes in grass and put them into the pit, on top of the newly dug camas. After this second steaming the cakes would be pounded again and then dried over the fire. These dried cakes, packed in dry grass, were light and easy to carry. They lasted a long time without spoiling and were very nourishing.

With the pit full and covered, the women and girls hurried to their homes to prepare for the ball game. The game was always played between two teams; usually men and boys were on one team, women and girls on the other. But at this spring gathering so many of the men were away that the people decided to have only the boys play on one team and only the girls on the other.

The field was a sandy stretch that separated the camas meadows from the river. It had not been completely leveled. There had not been enough time to do this with so many of the men away. The boys did burn off some of the brush and pull some of it out, to make sure a runner would not trip over a stump or a bush. The two teams changed sides frequently, to make sure that neither side was favored by better ground. The goals were at either end of the field.

The boys, wearing only breechcloths, raced for the field first, waving their long curved sticks that looked like hockey sticks. They took their places with their backs to the sun. The girls would have to face the sun. The boys hoped this would give them an advantage over the girls. Later they would change sides.

The girls came racing to the field soon after the boys. They took up their places, shading their eyes against the sun in order to look the field over and become familiar with it. To warm up, each team began to practice with old balls they had brought with them, swinging their sticks and racing back and forth. The balls were made of buckskin, stuffed with buffalo hair.

Men, women, and small children came straggling to the field singly and in two's and three's. Several of the women carried babies, some in cradleboards. Other women moved slowly toward the field, as fast as their three- and four-year-old children could walk. Slowly the edge of the field filled with people who wanted to see the game, some from other villages whose meadows were nearby. Everyone tried to find a place with the best possible view of both sides of the field. The audience whispered among themselves and placed bets after they had sized up the players. Many bet on the team their girl or boy happened to be on.

At last came the Peace Chief, who was to act as umpire. He stood in the center of the field and held up his hand as a signal for the players to get ready. He motioned to the audience to quiet down. Then he raised the small ball—a new one—and threw it high in the air.

The wind caught the ball and sent it toward the boys. The boys pounced on it. The line of girls closed and rushed forward to prevent the boys from getting the ball through them toward the goal. One of the girls pushed herself right into the circle of boys and struck at the soft ball with her stick. It rolled through the boys' legs and down the field toward the boys' goal. A shout, a cry of victory, rose from the girls as the goal was made.

Although the Nez Perce boys practiced running almost daily, the girls were just as swift. Sunflower Girl, especially, was as swift as an antelope. She seemed to float in the air. But the line of boys defending their goal stood firmly together, sticks ready. When the small ball neared

the goal, one boy whacked it back through the crowd of milling legs toward the girls' goal.

Disappointed, the girls whirled and raced down the field, trying to stop the ball and prevent the boys from scoring.

And so the game went on, back and forth, back and forth, up and down the long field. The shouts of victory or despair were now in the boys' voices, now in the girls' higher-pitched cries. Yet no one scored.

At one time a girl was about to score, but one
of the boys rushed up and tripped her. The girl
fell flat. Her stick rolled away in the sand like a
piece of tumbleweed. Several girls dropped their
sticks and came to her aid. They lifted her up
and brushed the dirt off her short skirt. Everyone
was shouting at the boys for unfair play. The ball
lay forgotten while the boys and girls on the two
teams fought a battle with fists and elbows and
hair pulling—the girls pulling the boys' long

hair. The boy who was the cause of the fight lay on the ground, being pummeled by several girls. He had covered up his face to protect his eyes and nose from the sand and from the soft moccasins that kicked him. He was pleading and laughing. The girl he had tripped was also laughing now.

The umpire went over and picked up the forgotten ball. Then he joined the people on the edge of the field. Everyone was enjoying the fight, laughing and shouting encouragement first to one side and then the other.

"She likes that boy," one woman said, "and he likes her. That's why he tripped her. Maybe he will marry her after this game. They are both old enough."

"We can have a marriage feast tomorrow," another woman began to plan.

"Her father has to return first," the girl's mother objected.

Now the Chief stepped out on the field again

and held up the ball, waiting for the players to line up. The field grew quiet. He threw the ball, and again the wind favored the boys' side. They rushed for the ball.

The sides were so well matched that neither, despite its efforts, succeeded in scoring even one point. This made them try all the harder. An outsider would not have suspected that they had been through a long day's work. The players had forgotten their fatigue.

When the sun reached the mountain rim to the west, the old Chief left the edge of the field, where he had been sitting, and held up his hand. He ruled that the game should end for the day.

It started again in the afternoon of the following day. The weather had turned windy and cloudy, but that did not stop anyone from attending the game. People brought their heavy robes and, having tucked themselves in, sat down to watch the contest.

The game started with a spurt. At first it

seemed that the boys would score, but the girls guarded the goal as intensely as they had the day before.

Suddenly Sunflower Girl whacked the ball. It arched over the boys' heads and fell close to the goal. Another girl had pushed her way through the line of boys and she gave the ball the final push, as it touched the ground. The girls had scored!

Now the game was really getting rough. The boys, imitating the girls' tactics, pushed through their lines and scored once too. With the score tied, each side renewed its efforts. The audience shouted encouragement. The boys fought hard, and scored two more points. But luck seemed to favor the girls. They scored again and again. When the score was five to three in favor of the girls, the Peace Chief called a halt. The sun was setting. Besides, five was a lucky number and it seemed good to leave the winning score at five and start the feast. People quickly collected their bets and moved toward the steaming pit, where the older women had uncovered the camas bulbs and put them into the serving bowls.

Spotted Salmon had been so busy playing and feasting that he had not thought much about his father, although Mother had made up Father's bed in their shelter. But that evening, after the game, someone shouted, "They are coming!" Several horsemen were racing toward the camp. Father had come home! With much rejoicing, families were reunited after months of separation. The newcomers were soon seated near the pit, and the feast of camas began.

Spotted Salmon could hardly eat. He had never seen Father look more handsome. He was wearing white buckskins with two scalps on his belt. Long, round dentalia shells were braided in his hair. A wide breastplate of dentalia covered his entire chest. Spotted Salmon looked at the heavily laden pack horses. Father had had a good trading trip.

3

BECOMING A CHIEF

Father remained in the village after the people returned from the camas meadows just long enough to unpack his horses and set the packs inside the longhouse. He examined the horsehair ropes Spotted Salmon had made and praised the boy for his fine workmanship. "That is how ropes for horses should be made," he said. "On the plains you can get anything you want for such ropes—plenty of hides and meat." With Spotted Salmon at his heels, Father went to look over the horses. Again he was full of praise for his son. "You have done a man's job, Son," he said. "As soon as Mother is ready, we will go back to the buffalo country to trade and to hunt. The old people can stay here with Brother's wife."

All that day they were busy with the herd, counting, sorting, and planning for the trip. Father asked Spotted Salmon again and again to catch a horse or colt for him. He was pleased

with the way the boy had learned to handle the lasso. "You must have practiced long, Son," he said. Spotted Salmon's joy knew no bounds. There were several things he wanted to say, but Father kept him on the run till sunset.

Inside the house, Mother had prepared the fire and had hot baking stones ready. She had thought the men were out hunting. In order not to disappoint her, Father opened a parfleche, a decorated buffalo hide that folded like an envelope. In it were several layers of stiff, dried buffalo meat. Mother took two pieces and put them into a basket pot of water heated with hot stones. She added dried camas. "This will make a tasty meal," she said, "but you will have to rest for a time while the food is cooking. There is enough meat in this pack to last us for a long time."

"We will use this meat for a feast later on, after the salmon comes," Father said.

Father had many relatives and friends in his own village and in the neighboring villages. He wanted to invite them to see the things he had brought back and to tell them of his experiences on the plains. Already Father's two brothers were on their way to the neighboring villages to invite people to this feast. Spotted Salmon was to go to the next village the following morning to invite a few of the young men there. He prepared a little bundle of thirty sticks, so the guests could count off the days before the feast. Meanwhile, much had to be done in preparation for it.

The people in the big house were all anxious to help, since everyone enjoyed a feast, no matter how hard they had to work preparing for it.

Spotted Salmon was aware that Father was introducing new ways he had learned from the Plains Indians. There, when a man gave such a feast and invited young men, it meant that he was aiming at becoming a war chief. Among the Nez Perce, a peace chief was usually selected by the entire village, from among several candidates. The people sat long in council, discussing each candidate—the way he behaved, the way he got along with his family, his relatives, and his friends. Each person in the council had a chance to voice his opinion of the candidate. The Nez Perce were very frank and outspoken in these councils. When the talk seemed to indicate definitely which man was the best for this re-

sponsible office and the best for the village, the
people voted.

Unless the vote was unanimous, however, the
man could not be elected. In our democratic
government a candidate has to be elected by a
majority vote. But among these Indians the person had to be chosen unanimously. Before calling
for a vote, therefore, a man's friends and relatives
made sure he would get all the votes. They frequently asked the council to adjourn for a few
days, while they went about convincing former
opponents to vote for their candidate.

To become a war chief, a man did not have to
be elected at all. His success as a leader and
warrior and his courageous and wise behavior
during raids were important factors. He became
a war chief if he had a large following of young
men who trusted his judgment and courage.
Spotted Salmon knew the reputation of the young
men his father singled out to invite to his feast.
He wants these men with him, Spotted Salmon
thought, not only to trade when they reach the

plains, but also to hunt buffalo. If they enter someone else's territory, they will be ready to fight. And Father will lead them on the warpath.

The Nez Perce had lived in harmony with their close neighbors, whom we call the Umatilla, the Yakima, and the Flatheads. When the Nez Perce first began to trade horses with the plains tribes they were welcomed by them, as well. But as time went on and some of the Nez Perce stayed on the plains and hunted buffalo themselves, instead of just trading horses, the Plains Indians began to war with them. And the Nez Perce men had never run away from a fight. There were always long periods of peaceful trading between the wars—much longer than the periods of fighting. The Plains Indians were not breeding enough horses and they depended on the Nez Perce to supply them with more horses for buffalo hunting.

When Spotted Salmon returned from his errand to the neighboring village, Mother and her two sisters-in-law were hard at work tanning the buffalo skins Father had brought back. Since there were always skins to dress, the women saved the brains and some of the fat whenever deer and elk were killed. They kept a mixture of brains and fat in a little hut near the longhouse. They added water to the mixture and rubbed it on the inside of the buffalo skins. Each skin was rolled up separately so that the mixture would be absorbed.

The next day Mother and her helpers began to work on one of the hides that had been treated with the mixture of brains and fat. They spread the skin on a thick log and began to scrape the fleshy side free of bits of flesh, veins, and skin that had stuck to it. This scraping, done with a sharp bone scraper, was a slow, tedious job. The women talked as they worked the robe.

A buffalo robe was usually embroidered with stripes of dyed porcupine quills or was painted with earth colors. A woman did not make up her mind at once about the design she was going to put on a robe or a dress, or on a shirt for her husband.

She let the shape of each skin, its particular color and texture, influence her thoughts about the design. When she finally set to work with her bowl of porcupine quills, her bone awl, and her sharp shell knife, the design suggested by the skin itself was firmly fixed in her mind. She went about embroidering the skin without making any mistakes. The Nez Perce women were known for their excellent work on skins and bags.

Because this buffalo skin was longer than usual, the women thought it would be best to paint designs on it. In painting a buffalo robe or a buckskin, a woman first mixed the colors she planned to use: red, blue, green, and yellow. Red and yellow were the favorite colors of the Nez Perce. These she painted on the robe with a brush made from a twig.

The scraping of the hide, even though three women worked at it, took all morning. Having finished scraping, the women rubbed in more fat to soften the skin. Then they turned it over and began to clean the matted hair. Two women held the hide. They placed it over a pole and pulled it back and forth till the dust and sand had been shaken out. Next they spread the hide out flat.

With fanlike combs made from sticks tied with buckskin thongs, and brushes made from twigs, they combed the matted hair. They trimmed and cut it. They washed the hair clean, till it shone brown and tan.

"This robe will be worth two horses," they said, admiring it.

Tired from the day's work, the women straightened their aching backs and stood outside for a while before they began to prepare the evening meal. Luckily Mother had tanned many buckskins last fall. Now she had only the sewing to do, while her sisters-in-law still had to tan buckskins before they could begin to make clothing. Tanning a buckskin was very much like tanning a buffalo hide, except that both sides of a skin had to be rubbed with the mixture of brains and fat, scraped, stretched, and then smoked. The smoking was done by draping the skin over a frame made of twigs and lighting a small fire under it. This fire gave out little heat, but much smoke.

A man's outfit took a long time to make. It consisted of a pair of leggings, a breechcloth, a belt, a shirt, and a pair of moccasins. The leggings extended from the ankles to the thighs, and the upper end of each legging was tucked into the belt. A man's breechcloth was made of a wide strip of buckskin. The strip was worn between his legs, with one end looped over the belt in front and the other in back. A man's shirt usually had long sleeves and was made out of two skins. There was an opening at the top. A man put on a buckskin shirt as we do a pull-over shirt. The seams on the sleeves and sides were edged with fringe. There were also rows of fringe on the shoulders and across the back and chest.

The more elaborate the costume, the prouder the wearer. Men liked white buckskin and so did the women. They kept their clothing neat and often rubbed the white buckskins with white clay to clean them. Quillwork in various patterns was embroidered across the chest, back, and shoulders, as well as on the sleeves. Often the entire front of a shirt was decorated with quills. A collar of otter skin, with the tail hanging down in front, was sometimes worn. Other men, like Spotted Salmon's father, wore wide breastplates of beads or shells. Men ornamented their hair with large beads and shells hung on leather thongs, pieces of fur, and feathers. Other favorite ornaments were necklaces of bear claws, eagle claws, wolf teeth, and deer hoofs.

Women's dresses were just as elaborate. Mother made her dress out of two full deerskins sewed together. One skin formed the front and the other skin the back of the dress. By folding the tail end of the skin on the outside, she made a sort of yoke. The dress reached to her ankles and hung straight from the shoulders. She did not wear a belt. Pieces of buckskin were added to the hem of the dress to make it even; and the seams, sleeves, yoke, and hem were decorated with fringe. The hair side of the skin was worn next to the body. Because it had been carefully scraped and smoked, the inside of the skin always looked better. Its texture was more even. A woman kept adding ornaments to her dress as long as she used it. She might start with quills along the yoke, and later add dentalia and ornaments made of rounded pieces of bone, copper, feathers, or hair.

For ceremonies boys and girls dressed like grownups. Otherwise, boys wore only breechcloths and moccasins, and girls wore short dresses and moccasins. Little children went about naked.

To keep her family and herself clothed, a woman spent much of her spare time sewing and mending clothing and moccasins. Little girls began to help their mothers with the sewing as soon as they could pull sinew through the little holes that Mother made in the buckskin. A woman's little wooden bowl always had deer or elk sinew soaking in it. She pulled out thread after thread as she worked. Sinew made execellent thread. It stretched when moist. As it dried it shrank and made the seams tight and the stitches very fine.

Both men and women wore caps. Men's caps were made of fur, buckskin, or hide. They fitted the top of the head like a crown. The back of a man's cap ended in a long flap, to protect the neck. Women's caps looked like baskets turned upside down. They wore these caps low over their foreheads. When they carried burden baskets, the

strap fitted over the cap, which protected the forehead. The women decorated their caps with colored quills and tassels. Both men and women wore their hair long, parted in the middle, and braided in two braids that hung over the shoulders. Only the men wore bangs.

The moccasins the women made were soft and close-fitting. The sole of a moccasin was cut the exact shape of a person's foot. The top, cut out of one piece of buckskin, was sewn onto the sole. A flap fitted around the ankle and was tied underneath with a thong.

The men were always as busy as the women. They needed bows and arrows for hunting and for trading. The Nez Perce were famed for their bows made of wood—yew, ash or willow. They scraped, smoothed, and soaked them. Then they bent the wood into an arc and tied the ends until it was dry and so would hold its shape.

But the bighorn sheep's curved horn made the best and most desirable bows. Such a horn bow was indestructible and would serve a hunter forever. No other bow could equal it for elasticity that always remained the same. It could shoot an arrow an amazing distance. People were ready to trade a horse or even a gun for a bighorn sheep bow.

The old men made these bows by splitting a large horn and taking one strip out. This strip of horn retained its spiral coil. It was then steamed, stretched, and straightened out until it was about three feet long. Then the maker wound moistened sinew around and around the strip of horn till the sinew was about a third of an inch thick. He glued this sinew to the bow with the blood of the winter steelhead salmon. This blood, scraped from the skin of the salmon, had been boiled and spread out on a rack to dry. It made excellent glue, and men kept chunks of it for use in making bows and arrows. All they had to do to use this glue was to moisten some of it with saliva and spread it on a surface. After the bow with the glued sinew dried, it was ready for use.

The old men also made arrowheads and shafts,

and the boys learned these skills by watching them. Men and boys gathered slender branches of the serviceberry for shafts. They made shafts about as long as a boy's arm. After removing the smooth, brownish bark, they heated these branches to straighten them. They polished the shafts and decorated them with painted bands. They glued feathers at the base or tied them on with sinew.

Arrowheads were of many shapes and sizes, depending on their use. Some had smooth edges, some rounded; some looked like triangles. The men flaked and chipped their arrowheads out of obsidian and flint. They made a notch in the shaft and fitted the arrowhead into it. Then they bound the shaft with moist sinew. As the sinew dried, it contracted and held the arrowhead tight within the shaft. Some men dipped their arrowheads in snake poisons to make them more deadly.

Nez Perce hunters were as quick with their bows and arrows as some of our modern experts are with automatics. A hunter held two or three extra arrows in his left hand while shooting, so he could shoot several arrows, one after the other. No man went anywhere without his bow and a quiverful of arrows. Although the women did all the sewing of clothing, the men sewed their own quivers. They used the skin of otter, coyote, or cougar to make quivers. The quivers were of the same length as the arrow shafts.

Of all the articles of trade, eagle feathers were considered most valuable by all Indians. Some time before the feast that he was planning, Father set out to get eagle feathers to present to his guests. The Nez Perce did not keep eagles in captivity. Sometimes, when boys raided an eagle's nest, they took a nestling home. After rearing it in the village, they plucked some of its feathers. When the feathers grew again they plucked the eagle a second time and then let it go.

Father and his two brothers and Spotted Salmon set out for a rocky ledge some distance from their village, where they knew eagles were

nesting. They dug a pit where Father was to hide, and laid a false surface of grass over it. They left a few openings in this false surface and tied a rabbit as bait.

Father did not have long to wait before a hungry eagle swooped down. As it landed, Father seized its feet and tied them. One brother held his bow ready and shot the eagle. As Father came out of the pit, his hands were bleeding from the eagle's claws, but he was happy. Now there would be enough eagle feathers for the young men invited to the feast.

All these preparations were being made to insure that the feast would turn out as planned. With Mother and Father so busy, Spotted Salmon still did not get a chance to speak to them about Sunflower Girl and ask Father for the white Appaloosa mare and her colt. He now wanted that horse more than ever.

He had seen Sunflower Girl several times when he was watering the horses and she came down to the river with another girl to fetch water. They spoke only a few words at first. Spotted Salmon was careful to say very little, because the other girl might tell Sunflower Girl's mother. It was not right for a young man to speak to a girl. He must speak to her father first and bring him a gift.

At one such meeting, Spotted Salmon rode another horse as he led the white mare to the water. Sunflower Girl put down her full water basket and watched. Spotted Salmon sat still on the horse, his eyes on the pretty girl.

Sunflower Girl started toward him. She came over shyly and put her small hand on the white mare's neck to pat her. "You have the most beautiful mare in the whole Wallowa Valley," she said.

Spotted Salmon almost blurted out the truth: "That mare is not mine. She belongs to my father." But he caught himself in time. After all, he had been caring for the mare for almost a year and had kept vigil through the chilly spring nights so her colt would not be harmed. Surely, when Father found out how much he wanted them, he would be pleased to make him a gift of this mare and her colt for all the work he had done. So Spotted Salmon said, instead, "Would you like to ride her? She is very gentle."

"I am not afraid," Sunflower Girl said.

Spotted Salmon slipped from his own horse and lifted Sunflower Girl up on the mare. She waited for him to remount and the two of them rode away from the river and circled around the village a few times.

The following day, when Spotted Salmon came down the river, Sunflower Girl was waiting there, with her basket full of water. Again he led the white mare over to her and lifted her up. Once more they rode for a short time before returning to the riverbank to pick up the full water basket.

Spotted Salmon would have liked these rides to go on forever. But they were interrupted by the coming of the salmon.

4

THE COMING OF THE SALMON

The coming of the salmon in *Hillal*, or June, provided the Nez Perce people with their most important supply of food. Through many months of the year, men and boys, women and girls, worked hard at their varied tasks of getting and preparing food. They did not, however, look upon these occupations as chores. Each brought with it good times. Whether the women and girls were digging camas or kouse roots, gathering berries or nuts, or cutting the heads of sunflowers for their seeds, they feasted, played games, and danced at the end of a day's work. Each evening, after a long, strenuous day of fishing, men and boys looked forward to a feast of broiled fresh fish and to the storytelling, games, and dances that followed these feasts.

When the dainty white flowers of the shadbush

unfolded, spring arrived for the Nez Perce villages. The children watched the berries forming on the bushes and then ripening into sweet, juicy fruits. They were not alone in this. Squirrels, chipmunks, and bears wanted these berries too, when they ripened. But berries grew in such abundance that there was enough for everyone. Women and girls filled basket after basket, and the children, after eating their fill, carried the baskets home on horseback.

Berries ripened in June and July. When Father was at home, he and Spotted Salmon and a few other men sometimes hid in the berry bushes, warning youngsters and women to keep away. When a bear came to feast on the ripe berries, they shot it and the entire village enjoyed a feast of bear meat. The women boiled the meat and saved the grease to use in cooking and in mixing paints.

There were many kinds of berries: buffalo berries or rabbit berries, blackberries and blueberries, cloudberries and salmonberries. Boys liked to hide in the bushes and shoot birds that came to feed on the berries and rabbits and deer that came to eat the leaves and stems of the young plants. Chokeberries, currants, gooseberries, and roseberries remained on the stems during the

winter and could be picked and eaten late in the year. Roots, such as bitterroot and wild carrot, were gathered and they were eaten either dried or boiled.

Walking or riding to and from their berry picking, women and girls always stopped to admire the yellow stretches of sunflowers that bordered the meadows and hillsides. At this time the sunflower heads—like giant eyes—were filling with seeds that would be ready for picking in

early fall. Sunflower seeds were another important food. The sunflower is an American plant,
a native of the great plains. Long golden patches
of sunflowers were another sign of spring on the
plateaus of the Nez Perce. The large, round
heads turned throughout the day to follow the
sun's journey across the sky, as though they had
eyes. The plant was aptly called sunflower.

Spotted Salmon noticed that before the sun
rose each morning the heads faced west, just
as the last rays of the setting sun had left them
the evening before. As the sun rose in the east,
the heads with their brown centers and yellow
petals, turned to face it and kept on turning until
at evening they faced toward the west again. The
heads grew heavier and heavier as the seeds
swelled throughout the wet spring and ripened
during the dry summer. They began to droop
with their own weight and the seeds were ready
for picking in early fall.

The cut sunflowers were allowed to dry before
the seeds were shaken out. Dry sunflower seeds

kept so well that many women simply stored the baskets filled with them. During the year, whenever Mother wanted to use sunflower seeds, she took a few handfuls, shelled them, and pounded the kernels into tasty, oily cakes, or boiled them in water.

The Nez Perce women neither planted the sunflowers nor gave them any special care. They merely left some of the seeds on the ground each fall. In the spring sunflowers came up.

The coming of the salmon in *Hillal*, or June, provided the Nez Perce people with their most important supply of food. Before the salmon actually came, men and boys rode along the river from time to time, looking for the rounded, shiny forms of the Chinook.

Because of his name, Spotted Salmon was sure he would be the first to spot the fish. The salmon favored him. When he was about ten he had gone up a nearby peak to seek a vision. In his dream a salmon leaped out of the Wallowa River over a mountain peak. The name *Spotted Salmon* was then given the boy by Grandfather. After he sang the song about his vision at a ceremony, everyone knew that he would be a successful fisherman when he grew up.

It was Mother's great disappointment that her son liked riding horses more than he did fishing. "It would have been different if we still followed the old ways," she said to her friends. "He likes horses even more than my husband does."

It had been the same every June, as far back as Spotted Salmon could remember. One day the river flowed peacefully between its high banks, the water carrying the usual debris: logs, broken twigs, bark. The next day the stream was full of the silverbacks, crowding upstream, and people were hurrying from the villages toward the water with fishing gear, nets, and traps to catch the salmon.

Once the run of salmon began, it was more exciting than any horse race. Feverish activity lasted through many days and nights. Men and boys, thrilled with the excitement of fishing, kept on day after day and, with the aid of torches, night after night.

Where did all this milling mass come from? To this day scientists still marvel, as the Nez Perce did for centuries, at the instinct that sends the salmon back, many years after their birth in these waters, to breed in them again, as their ancestors had done.

The Nez Perce legends had a ready explanation. It was all the doing of Coyote, their hero. According to one legend, Coyote lived on a mountaintop overlooking the Great Water, the Pacific Ocean. Once Coyote saw salmon swimming in the Great Water. He saw they were large and fat, and he thought they would make fine food for the people. So he ordered the salmon to swim up the rivers and streams of the Nez Perce lands and let themselves be caught. Because Coyote had planned this for the people, the Nez Perce made sure that they caught quantities of salmon and that none of it was wasted.

Like many other Indians, the Nez Perce gave

the name *salmon* to all the fish that came up their streams to spawn. The best and the largest of these was the Chinook, or king salmon.

This year, as the migration upstream started, the fish ran so thick that the people crowding on the wharves and fishing stands they had built scooped them up in large dip nets. They also used seines. These were very long nets, about twice as

long as a man is tall. The men attached logs to the seines to act as floaters and tied boulders to the net for sinkers.

Some of the men and boys built small dams and weirs across the stream. These weirs were made of brush and were placed in the stream, leaving a narrow passage. Some of the salmon were thus able to escape and swim farther upstream. This was done purposely, so the people living higher up the stream could also catch fish.

The younger men liked to station themselves on the wharves and spear the salmon. They made two kinds of spears. The length of the spear shaft was about one and a half times the height of a man. Some spears had bone heads with incised barbs attached to them. Others had a detachable spearhead. As the spear was thrown and hit its mark, the head became detached and the barbs stuck firmly inside the fish. The long cord connecting the spearhead and shaft trailed in the water. The fishermen held the shaft firmly in his grasp. After the fish stopped struggling, the man pulled in the cord and caught the fish.

Men also fished from their large dugouts. The Nez Perce hollowed these boats out of tall fir logs. The boats were flat-bottomed, so they were not easily tipped over. The sides were rounded and tapered toward the bow. Men hollowed out the boats by making a fire in the center of the log. As the wood charred, they scraped it away with

their stone and shell knives till the entire inside
of the log was evenly scraped away.

The men and boys worked hard at their fishing
posts. The older men encouraged the boys to try
harder, showing them better ways to throw a spear
and to recover it after it was thrown and the fish
was hooked. The same pride the older men took
when they killed a deer or a bear, the boys now
showed in spearing their salmon. They kept it up
hour after hour, forgetting their fatigue.

There were accidents, too—accidents that happened not only to the young and inexperienced,
but also to older men who had had much experience. Sometimes a man or a boy missed his footing
and fell into the churning, icy water to the amuse-
ment of his friends and relatives.

Spotted Salmon and Father were carried away
by the activity, as were the rest of their village.
They were now fishermen, not horsemen. They
stood at their accustomed place day after day,
getting their generous share of the fish.

Spotted Salmon carried to the village, on his

back, the first salmon Father caught. It weighed, he thought, about as much as he did, and it was as long as he was tall. The back of the fish was dark. Its sides, covered with dark spots, were silvery, like sunshine on the water. A beautiful creature, the boy thought. The fish opened and shut its mouth, gasping, then was still.

Spotted Salmon preferred warm creatures to these cold ones. There was more excitement in horses. He could control a horse and enjoy moving with it. He could never control a fish. Fish were made to be speared and eaten; horses for racing and adventure. Spotted Salmon had to help Father; they needed food for the feast. But he would have preferred to gallop over the plateau on Father's white Appaloosa, with her white colt racing after them.

In the meantime, while the men were fishing, the women and girls were preparing to take care of the catch. This was their job. Near each longhouse were drying racks built of poles. The women built fires under these drying racks. The boys carried up the fish from the river on their backs. The women cleaned and gutted them. Some were immediately impaled on sticks, ready

for broiling, so that the men would have hot fish when they came in from the river.

Fish intended for the drying rack were sliced in half along the backbone. The women removed the backbone and hung the fish to dry. All the women and girls could do during these feverish days was to clean and hang the fish. The actual task of drying would take place much later, after the run of the salmon was over. Each fish, after the initial drying, would be turned over and over till it was thoroughly dried. Salt they used only rarely. For the fish to be preserved and remain unspoiled from one season to the next, they had to be thoroughly dried, till they looked like brown boards. But these brown boards, when soaked overnight, with fish oil added, were quite tasty.

The women saved the fish oil to use in broiling the dried salmon, for flavoring, and in baking bread made from seeds or camas.

The salmon began to thin out. Most of the boys still remained at their posts. With the new skill they had gained from days of standing on the wharves and spearing the fish, they caught the stragglers that followed the enormous mass of salmon. This really called for skill. The boys worked together, throwing their spears one after the other. If one missed, another might get the elusive fish. At home there was enough fish to fill all the storage baskets. Yet they were reluctant to give up and take a well-deserved rest.

5

THE FEAST

Several days before the feast was to start, people began to come to the village. About twenty families from the neighboring villages finally gathered and put up brush shelters and tipis covered with skins and mats. Inside the shelters and tipis the people arranged their belongings: their baskets, blankets, robes, and dried food. The women and girls of each family went to the woods and brought back firewood, which they piled against one side of their shelter. Men stuck poles in the ground to which they tied their riding horses. The village boys took charge of the pack horses to see that they had plenty of grass. The visitors went hunting and brought back elk, deer, and rabbits. Some went down to the river to fish.

Spotted Salmon and his friends played host to the men and showed them the best places for fishing. They managed to get enough fish to broil for their evening meals.

On the afternoon before the day of the feast, it began to thunder and there was a strong wind. People expected it to rain. The women and girls rushed out, getting their cooking utensils and the blankets and baskets they had put outside to air. Others repaired the shelters, to make sure the mats and skins overlapped and were tight enough to withstand the storm. No one wanted his feast costume or food dampened and spoiled by rain. The rain came—a slow, steady drizzle that promised to last through the night.

Father worried about the rain. "It will spoil everything," he declared. "The horse races will not come off if the ground is wet and slippery. The horse races are the most important event. We cannot put things off too long. The people will run out of food and there will be no grazing left for the horses. The rain must be stopped!"

Father and Spotted Salmon went over to talk to Father's uncle, the shaman. Uncle was sure he had medicine powerful enough to stop the rain. He did not want to use this medicine, though, unless he received a very fine gift. "I am old," Uncle said. "Before I die, I want to own that white Appaloosa and her colt. I want to ride her to the feast."

Spotted Salmon was speechless. If only he had spoken to Father. Now it was too late.

"She is the best horse we own," Father said. "I wanted to keep her and raise more colts."

But Father pleaded in vain. Uncle wanted the Appaloosa.

"I will begin preparation for the rain ceremony as soon as you say the horse is mine," Uncle bargained.

Father gave in. "My son will bring the white Appaloosa to you tomorrow after the ceremony," he promised.

Spotted Salmon rushed out of the longhouse, fearing that Father and the shaman would see how upset he was. He wandered over to where the horses were grazing. The white mare and her colt looked pale blue against the gray sky. How beautiful they are, Spotted Salmon thought. I will not give them up. On an impulse, he put his best horsehair rope over the mare, whistled for his own Appaloosa, and started for Sunflower Girl's house, the colt following its mother.

Her family had just finished their evening meal. Spotted Salmon found a dry shelter and waited till everyone went to sleep before he called the girl's name. She heard him and came out.

In one breath he blurted out that he wanted her for his wife; that the Appaloosa was not his; that his father had not wanted to give the mare and the colt to his uncle, but that Uncle would not perform the rain ceremony otherwise. So Father had had to give in. Tomorrow the mare and colt would belong to Uncle.

"Come with me," Spotted Salmon urged the

girl. "I have the good horn bow and the arrows
Grandfather made for me. I know where we can
go, where we have friends that always welcome
our people. Eagle Claw told me about this village. It is not too far from here. I will hunt and
fish and we will raise a herd of Appaloosas of our
own. We will then return to our people if we
wish to."

Spotted Salmon lifted Sunflower Girl up on the
white mare. Her white buckskin dress looked
pale blue, like the color of the mare. "You are
both beautiful," Spotted Salmon exclaimed, as he
mounted his own horse. With the white colt
ambling behind them, the couple left their
village.

"Son must be out with the herd," Father said
in the morning, looking at Spotted Salmon's
empty bunk.

The drizzle continued. Uncle was ready for
his sweat bath, to cleanse himself for the rain
ceremony. He and Father started for the small
hut that was used for a sweat bath. The hut was

almost airtight. Inside was a firepit. Father built a small fire outside the hut and heated several stones in it. When the shaman entered the hut, Father put the heated stones in the firepit inside and poured a basketful of water over them. The hut soon filled with steam. The shaman sat inside, sweating. Then he ran out and plunged into the river.

Now, purified and cleansed, he went to the woods to work his medicine to stop the rain. The Nez Perce believed that a shaman could do this by means of certain songs and the medicine chants he owned. The shaman chose a tall pine. It stood alone on an elevation, so that when the tree was set on fire there would be no danger of the fire's spreading. Even though the ground was wet, it was safer not to endanger the woods by taking chances. Right beneath the tree, where the branches formed a dry spot, the shaman's helper lit the fire. It caught the base of the tree, and soon the tree was blazing.

Everyone in the village knew the shaman had

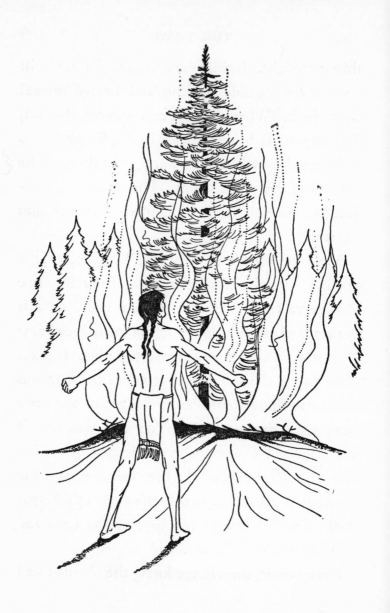

gone to the woods to stop the rain. They watched
the ceremony from a distance. It was too sacred
for anyone else to get too near. Soon the tree was
blazing and they could hear the shaman's voice
as he chanted his song, his head tilted back, as
though challenging the rain spirits to disappear.

As the shaman moved away from the blazing
tree and started back to the village, still singing
his song, the villagers were amazed to see a blue
patch opening in the sky. The rain began to cease
and a beautiful rainbow appeared behind the
blazing tree.

"We will have nice weather tomorrow for the
feast," the shaman promised. Tired from the
ceremony, he lay down on his bunk to rest and
sleep. He had not asked for the white mare and
her colt.

Now that the rain had stopped, the men
rounded up the horses they were going to race, in
order to prepare them for the event. A man
looked upon his horse as part of himself, and took
great care to have the animal look its best. Father

and his brothers were the only ones who owned saddles, which they had got by trading with the Crow Indians of the plains. Other men used blankets or rode bareback.

The men liked to streak their faces and bodies with red and yellow paint for these occasions, and they painted their horses with the same colors. From a distance a horse and its rider looked like one being. Sometimes the horse's tail was dyed red, while the mane was dyed black, or vice versa.

The Indians let their horses' manes and tails grow long and braided them, with feathers and leather. The feathers often stood up like a cockade above the horse's ears. They added more horsehair to the long tail. Sometimes they added so many long feathers and so much leather that the horse looked as though he had two tails. The tail swept the ground as the horse ran. Or the tail was clubbed into a knot and long streamers of feathers and leather were attached to it.

Having painted and decorated their horses, the riders, carrying their bows and arrows, aligned

themselves for the race—the first event of the day. First they stood facing each other in two long lines. Then one line of riders turned and rode away till they were almost out of sight. Whipping their horses to a gallop, shouting their war cries, the men came charging back toward their opponents. It took horsemanship and long training for the riders to remain seated as one line dashed through the other.

The people watching the contest were placing bets as to which line would win. The men charged, turned, and walked their horses back to their starting position. Those who had fallen off their horses during the charge left the line-up. Again and again they charged. The lines began to thin out till there were only a few left on either side. It was time to rest the horses.

The second event was a race. Scouts went out to mark the beginning and finishing lines for it. The winner was to get a buffalo robe which Mother had tanned. The men raced over uneven ground, past the village, up the hills behind the village, and were soon lost from sight. They reappeared again, as streaked specks in the distance, crossing the mountain creek and the meadows. After the winner received his prize the events were finished for the day.

Mother and her sisters-in-law brought out large wooden serving bowls filled with broiled fish, and bowls loaded with slabs of elk steaks and buffalo meat. The men sat in a circle with the dishes before them. Wives and children sat behind their husbands. The men helped themselves and passed some of the food to their families.

Mother had been so busy during the day cooking for the feast that she had had no time to think. But in the back of her mind she wondered and worried about Spotted Salmon. When Father could not find the Appaloosa mare and her colt that morning, after the rain ceremony, he had thought something must have happened to the horses and that Spotted Salmon had gone in search of them. Busy with his guests, Father could not leave the village to look for the boy.

Uncle was not at all concerned. Father always kept his promises. He had been too tired to ride the horse to the feast anyway, and he sat contentedly on the side lines with the other old men, watching the races. But he could not help boasting to his cronies about the mare and colt he now owned. "My Appaloosa could beat the whole lot of them," he said again and again. "Wait till you see her."

The feast over, Father lit a pipe and passed it around a few times. Everyone wanted Father to speak. The Nez Perce liked to listen to speeches. They liked the speakers to repeat themselves over and over again. Frequently another man, a younger one, stood right beside the speaker and repeated the speech sentence by sentence, imitating the speaker's voice and gestures. The audience liked this even more. It was important for a man who wanted to be a chief to be a good speaker, and Father was a good speaker.

As was the custom when speaking, Father stood up and pulled his robe about him. This

made him appear tall and commanding among the seated men. With the added bulk of the robe, he appeared even more impressive. Father freed his right arm so he could make appropriate gestures with it.

"Men and brothers," he began. All were silent as they smoked the pipe. Each puffed a few times and passed the pipe on to the person on his left.

Father said he had been away for a long time and now that he had come back he wanted all his friends to know what he had seen and experienced. If they were real men, they naturally liked adventure. They, too, could go out to the plains, to the land beyond the mountains, east of the rising sun, and see these things for themselves.

Some had already seen the buffalo herds. It was hard for those who had not seen game in such abundance to understand it. Flinging out his arm, Father indicated the immense stretches of plain covered with the large, heavy animals. "Meat for a land full of people!"

The horses owned by the Nez Perce were as a basketful of fish compared to those herds of buffalo. He had seen herds that covered the ground as far as the eye could see—where the sky met the earth. And all these creatures were there the year round, through spring, summer, fall, and winter. There was no need for anyone to suffer hunger, as the Nez Perce sometimes suffered hunger. On the plains there were always buffalo. "As long as we have our trusty Appaloosas, the best hunting horses, the people need never want food," Father said.

"Our brothers of the plains are not always ready to welcome strangers to their hunting grounds," Father went on. "That is why it is best for a large party of men to cross the mountains. A small party of three is unsafe. Anyone can attack a party of three. It has happened to others. After trading their horses, they had only their pack animals and their single mounts left. Later they were attacked by the same Indians with whom they had just traded. The rest of their horses were taken away from them, as well as the buffalo robes and other things they got in trade. A large party of warriors need have no fear of attack," Father concluded. "We need not fear entering any lands where there are buffalo."

Several other men were ready to speak now.

Each began by thanking Father for his hospitality. They were ready to go with Father at once, to leave their own lands and to make their home in the plains. The winter had been a hard one. They wanted no more hunger for the women and children. They would go with Father now.

Only a few men, the older ones, said they would not want to remain on the plains. But they would go along now. They were fishermen, and not wandering buffalo hunters. They did not want to give up the land of their fathers, this land of plateaus and winding rivers. They did not want to move into the lands of strangers, where they had enemies around them instead of relatives and friends, their own people. They would go with Father, but they wanted to come back here.

Father again got up to speak. "We will leave for the plains in a few days," he said. He, too, loved this land. He, too, wanted to come back, but he also wanted to enjoy the abundance of the plains. A large party of warriors could take their women along with them, to cook and dress skins.

Father looked about for Spotted Salmon. He expected to find his son behind him, as always. Instead, Mother sat alone, crying. Sunflower Girl's mother had told her that her daughter and Spotted Salmon must have run away together. Daughter's friend had told of their visits by the river.

Mother expected Father to be angry. Instead he seemed overjoyed. "That boy loved the Appaloosa mare and her colt," he said. "It upset me to have to give her away, because I could see how much the mare meant to him. But I promised her to Uncle and I must keep this promise. Tomorrow I shall take two horses over to Sunflower Girl's father. Let no one say my son failed to honor his marriage with a gift to his bride's father."

Mother felt as though a weight had been lifted off her shoulders. "Find out where they are," she begged.

"I will find them," Father promised. "Son and his wife will go to the plains with us."

Father's two brothers were now ready to perform. Each was naked, except for a breechcloth and moccasins. Each had painted himself for the warpath and carried his bow and arrows. The brothers stepped into the circle and began to dance a war dance. Their steps and chanting were strange to the Nez Perce. This war dance, Father explained, they had learned from the Crow. The three brothers had heard that the Crow were having a war dance. No strangers were allowed to attend this dance, so the three Nez Perce stole into the Crow camp at night, just as the war dance began. They lay in the grass all night, watching and listening to the Crow warriors. By the time dawn came, the Nez Perce had memorized the chants and dance steps. Since the Crow were mighty warriors, everyone believed that their dances and war songs were very powerful. Anyone who danced these war dances and chanted these songs would have the same great power on the warpath.

At first all the men watched the dance intently.

Then they got up, one by one, and began to practice it and chant with the brothers.

Father was happy because he had succeeded in convincing so many warriors. "On to the plains and buffalo hunting!" he shouted, as he joined the war dance.

The party turned out to be larger than Father had expected. Several more men from his own village joined him. A few days after the feast about twenty-five men took off for the plains with their wives and children. Father rode at the head of the party. He knew the trails, having been over them before. The men, carrying their bows and arrows, rode right behind him. The women and children followed the men. The boys were in charge of the pack horses, and they formed the rear guard of the party.

Spotted Salmon, riding his own Appaloosa, was in front with the men. During the first stretch of the journey, Spotted Salmon often looked back at Sunflower Girl, riding beside his mother on the white Appaloosa mare. He was happy over the turn of events and felt his guardian spirit had been with him. The young couple had been welcomed into the village where they stopped on the first night. Several men from that village were at the feast with his people. When Father came looking for the young couple a few days later, the village arranged a feast in honor of Father and Spotted Salmon and his bride.

When they returned to their own village, Spotted Salmon and Sunflower Girl, leading the white mare and her colt, went to see Uncle. Instead of being angry, Uncle said to Spotted Salmon, "You could have ridden the mare in the race if you had been here. I regret I did not ask you to do this before the feast. We might have won a few buffalo robes. I have more use for buffalo robes now than for a racing mare."

Spotted Salmon promised to get him buffalo robes on the plains, and Uncle handed the horsehair rope back to Sunflower Girl and told her to ride the mare to the plains.

The party moved slowly, for they were in no

special hurry. On the second day of the trip, most of the people were in country entirely new to them. They marveled at the new scenery, at the size and shape of the mountains, the deep valleys, the rivers; at the variety of plants and trees new to them. The women and girls set up their tipis each day as they did when going to the camas meadows. They took the packs off the horses and let them out to graze. The men hunted, and the boys went fishing whenever they camped near streams. After their simple evening meals there were games and dances. Some nights the men sat around the fires talking and the women sewed and mended moccasins by the fire-light.

A party with women and children was not regarded by other Indians with as much suspicion as a party of men alone, which might be a raiding party. At night Father posted scouts to watch the horses. He was not concerned about the safety of the camp. But horses were always a great temptation to raiding parties that might have sighted them during the day.

The band turned south after they crossed into what is now the state of Idaho and moved toward the Lolo Pass, which would take them across the Rocky Mountains into Montana and the plains.

As the days went by, the women and children began to tire of traveling. Their own homeland began to seem ever more beautiful, the pastures greener and more inviting. They all knew they would want to go back after the men had had

their fill of buffalo hunting and they had had their fill of buffalo meat.

They sighted the buffalo herd one day, toward evening. At first the herd looked like a black cloud on the horizon. As they warily approached it, the Nez Perce came upon a camp of Crow Indians. Father and a few of the men went over to talk with the Crow camp chief. As Spotted Salmon later reported to Mother and Sunflower Girl, they decided to begin trading horses in the morning and then the men would join the Crow for the buffalo hunt. They planned to run the buffalo over a cliff that lay farther to the south. All would share in the kill.

The women and girls set up their camp near the Crow camp. Mother and Sunflower Girl put some camas cakes into their best basket as a gift for the camp chief's wife, and went over to get acquainted and establish a path of friendship with the Crow people.

6

CHIEF JOSEPH SPEAKS

More has been written about Chief Joseph than about any other of the hundreds of Nez Perce chiefs who governed the fifty or so bands that made up the Nez Perce people. Most were able, intelligent, brave, and responsible men. Perhaps because Chief Joseph lived in turbulent times, his life was more in the public eye. Within a span of only twenty-two years (from 1855 to 1877) the Nez Perce, a free people, became reservation Indians. Joseph's life bridged this period.

He was born in 1840 on the Wallowa River in Oregon and died in 1904 at Colville Reservation in the state of Washington. As a boy, named

Heinmot Tooyalakekt, his life was very much like Spotted Salmon's, the son of a free people. He hunted, fished, feasted, and herded horses. His people were ready to welcome changes and to accept new ways. But they wanted to accept these new ways of their own free will and not have them imposed by others, by an alien government. Today we do not approve of a people's being deprived of their land by forced treaties. In the late nineteenth century, however, this was done.

Today perhaps, Joseph's fate and that of his people would have been a happier one. We have learned, at great cost of lives and property, to respect treaties and to respect the rights of people, even if the people are neither numerous nor strong. It is sufficient for us to know that they have needs. It was not so then, although the white man's contact with the Nez Perce began peacefully and remained so for half a century.

The first white men the Nez Perce saw were men of the Lewis and Clark Expedition in the year 1805. Meriwether Lewis and William Clark had been on the trail for over a year. They were on their way west to mark out the best route via the Northwest Territory to the Pacific Ocean. After they crossed the Bitterroot Mountains, they were in Nez Perce territory.

Up to 1805, the Nez Perce had not seen white men. They owned some metal tools, some knives, and even guns that white men had traded with the Indians to the east and that the Nez Perce eventually obtained in trade for horses. From these Indians the Nez Perce learned that white men were on their way toward the Great Water.

Young men who had been down on the Yellow-stone River returned and told their people that they had seen white men. These men, they said, had strange guns that held great power. A woman war captive told the Nez Perce that she had met white men and that they were very kind to her. These reports predisposed the Nez Perce to be friendly toward the Lewis and Clark Expedition, which had entered their lands.

It was at the time when the Nez Perce women went to the camas meadows. Since these strangers were peaceful, there was nothing to fear, no need to leave men to guard the villages while the people were away. At the meadows, several boys were lurking about the bushes, playing games, when they saw three bearded strangers. One of the strangers made friends with them. He gave them bands of red cloth and asked them to take him and the other two men to their camp.

The boys guided the strangers to the camp. There they were greeted as friends. Fish and camas were prepared for their evening meal and

the entire village gathered to look them over, touch them, and listen to them via sign language. The chief of the white men drew something on a piece of paper and asked a Nez Perce scout to take it to the place where the rest of the party waited for him. The scout was astonished to see that the man to whom he gave the paper knew just what his chief said.

After resting for several days the strangers asked for directions to the Great Water. The Nez Perce explained that they could reach the Pacific by going in dugouts down the Clearwater River to the Snake, and from the Snake to the Columbia. The Columbia River would lead them to the Pacific.

After this advice, the palefaces asked to have dugouts built for them. They lent the Nez Perce some of their metal tools—knives, hatchets, saws, and files. These tools cut so deep and clean into wood that the Nez Perce were amazed and immediately wanted to own them. In return, they promised to care for the Expedition's horses, and they showed Lewis and Clark a place to cache their other belongings until they returned from the Great Water.

Before the strangers left, they also presented the Nez Perce with medals and left a flag for an absent chief. At that time, some Nez Perce were away under the leadership of Broken Arm, fighting the Shoshoni, who had killed three of their men. On his return, Broken Arm took charge of the Lewis and Clark horses, and sent food to the Expedition when he heard the white men were in need. His own people at that time had little food. The winter of 1805 was unusually severe, and the Nez Perce felt sorry for these palefaces.

So began a friendly relationship between the Nez Perce and the whites. Once the Lolo Pass had been crossed by white men, more kept coming. Beaver, mink, and racoon abounded along the Nez Perce rivers and attracted fur traders. Unfortunately, many of these whites were ignorant of Indian customs. They kept asking the Indian hunters, who came to the American Fur Company post to trade horses for guns and powder, to get them beaver pelts.

Dressing pelts was women's work and the men did not do women's work. But the fur traders did not know this. They thought the Nez Perce men were too lazy to work, and they treated them badly. Because they suspected that the Nez Perce stole some of their goods, they raided their lodges. They did not know that the Nez Perce would not steal from friends.

Whenever the Nez Perce heard white men

sing, they listened carefully, hoping to learn some of their songs, as they had learned those of the Crow. Knowing a man's song gave great power. But even greater than the power of the guns and the songs seemed to be the white man's knowledge of how to read and write. The Nez Perce, who were always on the lookout for new things, wanted to learn this above all.

Twenty-six years went by. In the summer of 1831 the Nez Perce whom the Lewis and Clark Expedition had visited heard that William Clark was now in St. Louis, Missouri, as chief of Indian Affairs. At once three men started for St. Louis, a journey of some two thousand miles. They wanted to ask Clark to send them a teacher, so they could learn to read and write. Clark promised the chiefs to do what he could.

A missionary team, the Reverend and Mrs. Henry H. Spalding, finally reached the Nez Perce people in 1836 and settled in Lapwai. Mrs. Spalding immediately began to learn Shahaptian so she could translate some prayers into their language. Later she devised a special Shahaptian alphabet for them.

Every Nez Perce wanted to learn this powerful white man's medicine. To them it seemed as powerful as foretelling the future. Here, by means of a few lines on paper, one was able to tell another person's unspoken thoughts. No one was too young or too old to learn this. The sheets of paper with the alphabet that Eliza Spalding distributed to her school were taken home. In every home now, the evenings were spent in learning the alphabet and reading the simple sentences on the sheets, instead of in the usual storytelling.

In a very short time the entire village was able to read Shahaptian. This knowledge spread just as quickly to the other villages. The younger people were also gradually learning to read English and the Bible.

Unfortunately, the Spaldings were not content to stop with teaching the Nez Perce to read. They felt that it was necessary to teach these Indians to change their ways. First, the Spaldings objected because the Nez Perce children were out of school for months at a time in spring and fall, to go to the camas meadows. Boys, they felt, should remain in school to study and should not go fishing, or tend their fathers' horses, or hunt. The Spaldings tried to force the men to cultivate small garden patches. The men refused to work in the gardens. They liked to move about. It bored them to remain on one patch of ground, digging, weeding, and hoeing.

Many years later, a shaman named Smohalla, who wanted the Nez Perce to get rid of their white teachers, and indeed, of all the whites, put the thoughts of all the Nez Perce into words. "My young men shall never work," he said. "Men who work cannot dream, and wisdom comes to us in dreams. You ask me to plow the ground. Shall I take a knife and tear my mother's bosom? You ask me to dig for stone. Shall I dig under her skin for her bones? You ask me to cut the grass and make hay and sell it, to be rich like white men. But dare I cut off my mother's hair?"

But the Spaldings insisted. If the Nez Perce were to enjoy the school and learn the hymns, which had great power in them, they must obey their teachers, tend their own gardens, and cultivate the Spaldings' gardens and fields as well. The Nez Perce families who worked for the Spaldings neglected their own homes, their trips to gather camas, their hunting and fishing. They began to depend on the missionaries entirely. Faced with increased responsibilities, the Spaldings made even more rigorous demands. Men must not gamble. They must give up their horses. They must stay home and work the fields.

In 1836 the Spaldings estimated that there were between three and four thousand Nez Perce. Thirty years earlier Lewis and Clark had estimated that there were about six thousand. The Nez Perce villages scattered along the creeks and rivers numbered close to fifty.

As more and more white men came to the region, they brought diseases hitherto unknown to the Nez Perce. The worst of these were measles, smallpox, and scarlet fever. These maladies were fatal to the Indians, who had built up no immunities to them, and they died by the thousands. Whole villages were wiped out.

Following their ancient belief that a person fell sick because something entered his body, the Nez Perce shamans attempted to cure measles and smallpox by sucking out the foreign object from the invalid's body. They also tried to cure such diseases by means of chants and sweat baths. But the people died. The shamans reasoned that the white man's diseases were more powerful than the Nez Perce medicine. Some Indians accepted the white man's medicine, whenever it could be obtained, and some were cured.

To add further to the Nez Perce troubles, the winter of 1846-47 was very severe. The Spaldings did not have enough food for all the Indian families, who, having none themselves, came begging for it. The whites ate some of their horses, but the Nez Perce could not bring themselves to touch horseflesh.

The Federal government continued its efforts to get the Nez Perce into reservations. First, they tried to induce the Nez Perce to make treaties. For an agreed sum of money they were to give up their lands and retire to a reservation. There the United States commissioners hoped they would be unable to harm white settlers. While negotiating with the Indian chiefs for a treaty, the commissioners had troops parade on the council grounds, hoping to frighten the Indians into submission.

The first important treaty with the Nez Perce was made in the summer of 1855. Fifty-eight chiefs signed this treaty, among them Chiefs Lawyer and Looking Glass. They agreed to accept the limits of their lands as shown on the map. The lands included the Clearwater, the Salmon, the Snake, and the Grande Ronde Rivers and their valleys.

As Chief Joseph the Elder, Chief Joseph's father, had prophesied, the whites did not obey the land limits set up by this treaty. Instead, they kept encroaching on the Nez Perce lands. The situation became even more tense when gold was discovered in Idaho, in 1859. History tells us that an eighteen-year-old girl led the miners to the spot, in the Pierce City region. The rush that followed was like the California gold rush a decade earlier, although the Idaho gold deposits were inferior to those of California. But within three years the population of that part of Idaho increased to thirty thousand. Another gold discovery followed in the Boise River basin. It zoomed the population to forty thousand.

The miners were accustomed to treat Indians cruelly. The government agents, afraid of bloodshed, advised the Nez Perce not to insist on their rights. "Let these white men trespass," they told the Indians. "These miners merely want to get gold. They are not interested in land." The Nez Perce agreed to let the miners enter their lands. The miners promptly broke the agreement by trampling over the Indians' fields and stealing their horses.

When the Indians complained, the agents

asked them to give up more land and sign another treaty. The Indian chiefs asked the government to enforce the first treaty, made in 1855. The agents said they could not enforce it. "Then how do you plan to enforce the new treaty you ask us to sign?" the Nez Perce replied.

Most of the chiefs, among them Joseph, refused to sign any treaty. They held a council and agreed among themselves to follow the old custom. Let each chief be responsible for his own group.

The persistent commissioners, however, got fifty-one people to sign a new treaty in 1863. The men who signed this treaty were not chiefs and had no right to speak for the people. The treaty left the Nez Perce less than a fifth of the lands that remained to them under the 1855 treaty. The Nez Perce, therefore, refused to recognize the 1863 treaty.

On his deathbed, in 1873, Chief Joseph's father's last words were: "My son, always remember that your father never sold his country. You must stop your ears whenever you are asked to sign a treaty selling your home. Never forget my dying words. This country holds your father's body. Never sell the bones of your father and mother."

Young Joseph was thirty-one when he became chief of his village. Joseph claimed that the lands bordering the Wallowa River, the Wallowa Lake in Oregon, and the Imnaha River were his people's domain. On June 16, 1873, the President of the United States signed an order setting aside part of the Wallowa Valley as a hunting reserve for the Nez Perce. But the area he set aside was less than half of what Joseph claimed for his people. Joseph refused to obey the order. He wanted to go to Washington to see the President, but the local agent would not let him.

Two years later, in 1875, came another order from the President. The Wallowa Valley was declared open to homesteading. The Nez Perce were ordered to go to Lapwai. The Lapwai Indians protested. They said the Lapwai reservation was already full and could not hold more people. The whites ignored this.

Monteith, the Indian agent for that region, thought of other ways than the use of force to make the Indians come to Lapwai. He wanted to take away their horses, so they would become entirely dependent. He also wanted to take away their right to go to the camas meadows. He had troops ready to enforce these wishes. Finally, Monteith gave Joseph and his people thirty days, to April 1, 1877, in which to move out peaceably.

Joseph pleaded that he had to get his people to agree to move. They were ready to go on the warpath, and Chief Joseph wanted to avoid war. He said over and over again: "War can be avoided. I want no war. My people have always been friends of the white men. We cannot get ready in thirty days. It will take us that long to round up our scattered stock. Besides, the Snake River is now high with the spring waters. It is too dangerous to cross it. Let us wait till fall."

But the agents insisted that the Nez Perce

move immediately. These people had moved before, but at a time and speed they themselves
chose. This moving was not like going into the
camas meadows or on a winter's hunting trip.
Then the old people and the sick and the young
could be left behind in the winter villages. This
move was to be permanent. They could not cache
anything and hope to return later to pick it up.

The people began to pack their belongings. At
this time of year the Imnaha River crossing was a
quarter of a mile of icy, turbulent water. The
river had to be crossed by the old, the sick, the
children—as well as all the other people—and
the horses and cattle. The men made rafts of
skins and loaded the packs on them. They took
off their clothes and grabbed the ropes attached
to the rafts. They started racing their horses
before they got to the steep banks, so they would
be unable to stop before plunging into the icy
water. After many anxious hours the entire Wallowa band of the Nez Perce people had crossed
the Imnaha. The worst of the journey was over.

But a young man whose father had been killed by the whites was taunted by some of his companions, because he had failed to avenge his father's death. In anger, the young warrior called upon his friends for help. They left Chief Joseph's camp at night.

To avenge the young man's father, they killed the first four white men they met the next morning. General Oliver Howard immediately set out to avenge the four whites the Indians had killed.

The Nez Perce chiefs begged Joseph to run north to Canada and leave his country. Joseph's reply has become famous in history. "What are we fighting for?" he challenged the chiefs. "Is it for our lives? No. It is for this fair land where the bones of our fathers are buried. Some of you tried to say once that I was afraid of the whites. Stay here with me now and you will have plenty of fighting. . . ."

The fighting went on through the summer and the fall. It might have lasted even longer if Joseph had not been captured by General Miles under a flag of truce. But Joseph was tired by that time. His people, now less than five hundred in number, were exhausted.

On October 4, 1877, General Howard promised to let them return to Lapwai at once if they laid down their arms. Joseph was holding a war council with the remaining Nez Perce chiefs. Some still held out in favor of continuing to fight. Others wanted to leave the country rather than go to live on a reservation. But Joseph convinced them that it was best to surrender.

His message, in Shahaptian, was translated into English for the waiting United States Army officers. This speech has since become almost as well known as Lincoln's Gettysburg Address. It is certainly quoted as often. It is the dignified, simple, heart-rending statement of a defeated yet brave people. No one can read Chief Joseph's speech without determining to do his utmost to prevent such a thing from happening again either here in our nation, or elsewhere among other nations of the world.

"Tell General Howard," Joseph said, "I know his heart. What he told me before, I have in my heart. I am tired of fighting. Our chiefs are killed. The old men are all dead. It is the young men who say yes and no. He who led the young men is dead.

"It is cold and we have no blankets. The little children are freezing to death. My people, some

of them, have run away to the hills and have no
blankets, no food; no one knows where they are
—perhaps freezing to death. I need time to look
for my children and see how many I can find.
Maybe I shall find them among the dead. Hear
me, my chiefs. I am tired. My heart is sick and
sad. From where the sun now stands I will fight
no more forever."

The army did not capture all the warriors.
Some, led by White Bird, slipped away quietly in
the night and crossed the border into Canada.

With the Nez Perce beaten, our government
changed its mind. Instead of waiting till spring
and returning them to Lapwai, as promised, the
commissioners thought it would be cheaper to
feed the captives elsewhere. So another trek
began. This time the Nez Perce were sent to Fort
Lincoln, near Bismarck, in what was then Dakota
Territory. Some of the women and children, the
sick and the very old, were placed on fourteen
flatboats and taken down the Yellowstone River.

Those who could walk started the march overland.

From Dakota Territory, the Nez Perce were moved to Fort Leavenworth, in Indian Territory. The climate in this part of the country did not agree with the Nez Perce. Many of them died. However, even though they longed to return to their homeland, the remaining men and women began to cultivate farms. They soon had gardens, hay fields, chickens, sheep, cattle, and horses.

In 1879 Chief Joseph's autobiography was published. Readers of the book, and people who read newspaper accounts of how the Nez Perce had been treated, demanded that they should be returned to their homeland. In the face of this public demand, several widows and orphans were allowed to return to the Lapwai reservation. Three years later the rest of the people were moved. About two hundred were sent to Lapwai. The remaining one hundred and fifty, including Chief Joseph, were sent to Colville Reservation, in Washington. There Chief Joseph died nineteen years later, in 1904. Today some of the descendants of these Nez Perce still live in the Colville and Lapwai Reservations. Others have left the reservations and have scattered among their white neighbors.

Index